D0612117

Lent

An Uncommon Love Story

Lent

An Uncommon Love Story

By Antoinette Bosco

auline
BOOKS & MEDIA
Boston

Library of Congress Cataloging-in-Publication Data

Bosco, Antoinette, 1928–

  Lent: An Uncommon Love Story / by Antoinette Bosco.

    p. cm.

  ISBN 0-8198-4514-0

  1. Lent. I. Title.

  BV85.B64 2005

  242'.34—dc22

                                          2004014511

The Scripture quotations contained herein are from the *New Revised Standard Version Bible: Catholic Edition,* copyright © 1993 and 1989 by the Division of Christian Education of the National Council of the Churches of Christ in the U.S.A. Used by permission. All rights reserved.

Cover art: Pesellino, detail of *The Crucifixion with Saint Jerome and Saint Francis,* Samuel H. Kress Collection, © 2000, Board of Trustees, National Gallery of Art, Washington, D.C.

All rights reserved. No part of this book may be reproduced or transmitted in any form or by any means, electronic or mechanical, including photocopying, recording, or by any information storage and retrieval system without permission in writing from the publisher.

"P" and PAULINE are registered trademarks of the Daughters of St. Paul

Copyright © 2005, Daughters of St. Paul

Published by Pauline Books & Media, 50 Saint Pauls Avenue, Boston, MA 02130-3491.

Printed in U.S.A.

www.pauline.org

Pauline Books & Media is the publishing house of the Daughters of St. Paul, an international congregation of women religious serving the Church with the communications media.

1 2 3 4 5 6 7 8 9   11 10 09 08 07 06 05

I dedicate this book to my three sons,

Peter, John, and Sterling,

who blessed my life while on earth,

and bless me still from

the home they now share

with the Lord Jesus in heaven.

Contents

Introduction

Lent was never the season that won a popularity contest with me. I thought of it as a time of deep purple when Christians should focus on sacrifices, remembering that we are made of dust...and on and on. It was tolerable, though, because it was a preparation for the wonderful event of Easter, the celebration of Jesus' resurrection from the dead.

In contrast, the name "Easter" had a light, mysterious tone to it. The word comes from the Germanic "Eostre," meaning the dawn of a new day, and it was chosen by the early Christians who saw the rising light of a new day as a symbol of Jesus rising from the dead. The word itself was a tremendous expression of hope—that God had created a world of freedom, that people on this earth can aspire to "escape" and "resurrect," finding new, free lives.

But oh, the trials and pains along the way—and that's where Lent came in. There is no rebirth without pain, no resurrection—no Easter—without first the trauma of death.

That may sound dramatic, but whose life is spent without a lot of mourning? Consider the child felled by an illness; the innocent killed in political holocausts and bloody wars; the parent degenerating into senility; the depression at a discomforting passage in life; the loss of a job; the break-up of a relationship; the drying up of faith; the death of ideals, innocence, of hopes and dreams.

Why does it have to be this way? Why do we have to suffer the Lenten seasons and the Good Fridays? Why can't things be easier?

I don't know. If I knew the answer, I would be the greatest sage in the world. All any of us have to go on are the clues we get from our traditions—like Passover and Easter—events in which the mysteries of life are contained.

Most of the time, because we are mere human beings, we see through a glass darkly. We stumble along trying to understand the mysteries of pain, with no brilliant visions of eternity to help us along. The uncomfortable, annoying, miserable, traumatic, and tragic are built into human existence. And we protest because our human nature expects and desires that the self and the ego will never be put out. The clear message of Lent and Easter is that the self and the ego have to be jolted or we never come fully alive. That's both hard truth and mystery.

Back in the '80s I had the chance to interview Tom Jones, the man who wrote the lyrics for the musical, "The Fantasticks." I had always been impressed with the wisdom in his prize-winning song, "Try to Remember," especially the line, "Without a hurt, the heart is hollow." During our conversation he confided that he had learned that truth from his own pain, and then added that it was this truth that made life worthwhile. For without the dark side, we would never be able to appreciate the light, he said, paraphrasing what the saints have preached down through the ages. And I recalled what someone once wrote: "A clay pot sitting in the sun will always be a clay pot. It has to go through the white heat of the furnace to become porcelain."

And there is yet another perspective on human pain that makes sense to a person who believes in Easter. It was spoken by the writer, Oscar Wilde, who asked, "How else but through a broken heart can the good Lord enter in?" He implied in his very question the necessary ingredient for attaining this intimate relationship between us and the heavens.

I remember reading about Moorehead Kennedy, Jr., who had been held hostage in Iran for 444 days, and who spoke about the spiritual change he and his wife had experienced as a result of this traumatic experience. The theme of his message was that the fearful, long months of captivity had led each of them to a deeper spiritual transformation. Mr. Kennedy compared his personal crisis to Lent and Easter—Christ's suffering, death, and resurrection. Lent was the personal crisis, the "burning," but Easter was the proof that "we matter and we live."

Mrs. Kennedy likened the ordeal to a "crucible of anguish," a time for burning out the residues of this world—all the false values and the distorted desires of the ego—that envelop our lives with trash. Without the time for burning, the clutter would keep us immobilized, unable to move along in the faith-journey that leads us to God and life forever.

From the "crucibles" of my own life, specifically the deaths of three beautiful sons, I understood and related to the truth of what Kennedy said. For I have come to see Lent as the mosaic of what life is about. It is given to us as a gift to take an incredible journey of some forty days where we can gain moments of real insight, unlocking the mysteries of why life is as it is. In Lent, we are given the freedom to ask questions and cry out our confusions, trusting that God understands, because of the promise that was shouted from the cross: *You, my people, will not have answers—but something much better: life forever.*

In the chapters that follow, I offer my own vision of Lent, trying to take away the crusts, the negatives, the emphasis on sacrifice—sometimes artificial sacrifice—that sadly became the context in which I used to approach Lent. I hope my stories and reflections will encourage all you who read them to focus on your own lives and your stories. In our daily lives we have distractions, pitfalls, and so many happenings that make us feel that we are loners. Lent arrives to show us how wrong we are. Lent is a love story—an *uncommon* love story—showing us that, for all our difficulties and sorrows, we are not alone. We are forever linked to Jesus

Why We Need Lent

"The extreme greatness of Christianity lies in the fact that it
does not seek a supernatural remedy for suffering,
but a supernatural use for it."
— *Simone Weil*

In the Gospel of St. Matthew, Jesus tells us a story:

> Then Jesus was led up by the Spirit into the wilderness
> to be tempted by the devil. He fasted forty days and
> forty nights, and afterward he was famished. The
> tempter came and said to him, "If you are the Son of
> God, command these stones to become loaves of
> bread." But he answered, "It is written, one does not
> live by bread alone but by every word that comes from
> the mouth of God" (4:1-4).

The story goes on about how the devil did not easily
give up taunting Jesus. The evil one tried desperately to get

Jesus, in his weakened condition, to betray the Father and listen to him instead, to worship him and accept his satanic power—a power that can be so seductive when it comes with the lie that one's sufferings will end. Jesus answered him, showing us the way we are saved from evil: "Away with you, Satan! For it is written, 'Worship the Lord your God, and serve only him.' Then the devil left him and suddenly angels came and waited on him" (Mt 4:11).

This story tells us why we need Lent. As we join Jesus in his confrontation with Satan, this—his Lent experience—unlocks the mystery of why we suffer. Because of Jesus' trials and victory over Satan in the desert, we learn that our sufferings are not a terrible test but a reality of life, and that *Jesus'* victory can be *our* victory. When the angels comfort Jesus, that is our sign that God understands and has empathy for us. God will not abandon us.

We each learn this in our own way, out of the happenings of our own lives. For me, the experience of being divorced and the single parent of an older adopted son and six young children forced me to examine my values, my faith, and the very meaning of spirituality in my life—in detail akin to atom-smashing. When we are so immersed in problems, incessant work, daily confronta-

2 *Lent: An Uncommon Love Story*

tions with prejudices and other assorted pains, we can't really rest, or sometimes even pray, until we reach some clarity as to why life is the way it is.

For a while after my divorce, I descended into a sense of gloom about living. I continually cried out, *Who needs all this work and suffering?* Anyone suffering deeply can easily lose faith in life itself because the mysteries of living in times of profound suffering are too often wrapped in darkness. It is hard in troubled, painful periods to believe that the "good news" of religious faith is a valid message.

During that time, I used to say to myself, *I'm in the season of Lent, the long dark days in the desert.* Sometimes I wanted to scream for release, and that release could have been either/or: either an Easter and a new life, or, strangely and sadly, an eternal Good Friday that would bring unconsciousness and release from pain. I prayed desperately for help from the Lord and was given to understand there would be only one place to find hope: the desert, the place where we meet Christ courageously facing his own painful destiny.

That's not to say that I—or anyone—can truly understand the "why?" of earthly pain and loss.

Lent is a bridge between the two earthy worlds we straddle. On the one hand, we yearn for comfort, security, acclaim, attractiveness, good health, and knowledge. On the other hand, what we face—some periodically, some continually—is loneliness, illness, tragedy, anger, work, fear, boredom, and unexpected disruptions.

Meeting Jesus in the desert, we can cry out our confusion, believing that God understands, because we're standing there alongside his Son. With Jesus at our side, we can, as he did, move into a crucial acceptance of our own cross, believing that it is all right if we don't get answers to our questions about the tears in our lives. For we're going to have something much better: life forever.

In the desert, we meet our God with a human face. We confront evil. We're given the challenge to accept or to reject the cross. Christ said, "If any want to become my followers, let them deny themselves and take up their cross and follow me" (Mt 16:24). Clearly, he is telling us that "only by bearing one another's burdens do we fulfill his law," as the late Rev. Ralph W. Sockman wrote. He further explains:

> You take up your cross when you go the second mile beyond the point where duty and decency compel you. You take up your cross when, for the sake of some high ideal, you endure suffering which could have been escaped by a lower standard. You take up your cross when you sacrifice your own comfort to serve the needs of your fellow men or risk unpopularity to fight for the rights of others....

And with Christ's example of compassion before us, we cannot call ourselves his followers if our hearts do not go out to the world's sufferers....

Lent, indeed, is about carrying our cross, but it is not about imposing artificial "hardships," nor is it about self-focus. It is about linking ourselves with Jesus to the point that we are willing to become "another Christ" so that the work of bringing his Father's word to all continues until the end of time. Lent is the gift that assures us we are never alone if we "put on Christ" and live by all he taught us.

In the desert, Jesus said, "Away with you, Satan!" I believe these were the most powerful words ever spoken. He knew he needed to get on with his acceptance of "for this was I born," even if it meant enduring an agonizing passion and death. Yet, before this, he had work to do: to bring his love—the love of his Father—and the promise of life forever to all ever born: past, present, and to come.

Lent—the forty days in the desert—was the beginning. For the next three years Jesus would work full time to show us how much he loves us, and how much joy will be ours if we live faithful to the teachings he brought, which were the words—the truth—of his Father.

What began in Lent took root in the next three years and ended in brilliance. The British author, G. K. Chesterton, a convert to the Catholic faith, expressed this beautifully:

> On the third day the friends of Christ coming at day-break to the place found the empty grave and the stone rolled away. In varying ways they realized the new wonder; but even they hardly realized that the world had died in the night. What they were looking at was the first day of a new creation, with a new heaven and a new earth; and in a semblance of the gardener God walked again in the garden, in the cool not of the evening but the dawn.

I learned long ago that Lent is a bridge between the two earthy worlds we straddle. On the one hand, we yearn for comfort, security, acclaim, attractiveness, good health, and knowledge. On the other hand, what we face—some periodically, some continually—is loneliness, illness, tragedy, anger, work, fear, boredom, and unexpected disruptions. We can get lost in this maze of "earthiness"—witness the endless varieties of feel-better pills purchased daily by people, promising escape from life's depressing realities. Lent shows us the only reality that matters in the long run: the truth of God's love, in the person of his Son.

In that desert, where Jesus voluntarily went to pray and fast, Jesus saw the road ahead of him. When his Father asked him if he could take it, Jesus said yes. He willingly took on the pains—the sins—of the world to prove that he and the Father were *one* with all of us. Not only does this mean we can never accuse the Lord of true insensitivity to our pain, whatever it may be, it also means he feels our pain with us. He even has given us a roadmap for heaven: the assurance that his Father's love never ends.

But then there comes the confusion, the terrifying confusion emerging from unwanted blows that bombard us with a pain so severe that it cannot be defined: like surviving the death of a loved one, or an accident that destroys the body, or a brain malady that destroys the mind, or a hurricane that leaves a family naked. I could go on, but I don't have to. Pain spares no one.

The greatest suffering I have had to endure is the loss of three sons.

My youngest, Peter, suffered for nearly eleven years with an acute chemical deprivation illness in his head, variously diagnosed as severe schizophrenia or a bipolar malady. Peter killed himself at age twenty-seven; he wrote that he could no longer endure the pain and wanted to "go home," quoting C. S. Lewis that "earth is not our permanent home." Two years after this, my son John and his wife Nancy were murdered as they slept in their newly purchased home in Montana. And most recently, as I was writing this book, my son Sterling died after a heart and kidney transplant failed.

I have so often thought of Jesus' mother Mary, who also must have asked as I have after each of my children's deaths, *Why does my son have to die?* I believe that God must have agonized, too, as he watched his Son die.

I've heard it said that the loss of a child is "an impossible pain." And indeed, I was tormented that my sons had their lives cut off in such tragic ways. They all gave so much and still had so much to give when they died. I was overpowered by the realization that what happened to my sons was out of my control. I had protected them, nurtured them so constantly when they were growing up, but I had not been able to protect them from their tragic fates. I felt so flawed. But even harder to bear than my own guilt was the loss of their presence. How I missed them, and miss them still! I just want so desperately to hug them again. I think of them, and can feel the familiar weakness come over me—I am bleeding internally, the life draining out of me.

No one can be left "unchanged" after undergoing severe suffering. Pain can bring one closer to God or leave one very removed from him. I found truth in what the late author and Congresswoman Clare Booth Luce wrote, reflecting on her life before becoming Catholic:

> Grief has a purgative value, since God cannot fill the soul until it is emptied of trivial concerns. And a great grief is a tremendous bonfire in which all the trash of life is consumed. ...Grief gives man the opportunity to make Job's gift to God: the gift of his trust in ultimate goodness, when he seems most to be the victim of evil.

Truly, my pain dissolved my "trivial concerns," and my faith became stronger even though I had no answers for why we have to endure so much pain, wickedness, evil, sorrow, and destruction during life. I found I could be strong in my faith so long as I held tightly to the hand of Jesus, who didn't always have immediate answers himself, either, as evidenced when he asked, "My God, why have you forsaken me?"

Lent: An Uncommon Love Story

After each tragedy, I somehow accepted that faith was mystery and hope was uncertainty, because I had what was real—love. Nothing could take away the love that had been given to me in the very act of my being created, and the love that I was gifted with through all the people who ever touched me. To me, it became as clear as a sunrise that love never dies. I had Jesus' word for that. So I have learned that the only thing separating me from my loved ones is time. They are in eternity while I still live by the clock, but we are always together, and, one day, I shall be on the other side, with them again.

Perhaps because I had taken a Lenten journey with Jesus, a journey assuring me that love conquers death, my pain did not isolate me from God even though I was spiritually anguished. What surprised me even more was that, in my memories of my sons, joy always transcended sorrow. In feeling this joy, I was assured that I am connected to something larger than life, something utterly magnificent—God.

I remember one day talking in prayer to my son Pete. I asked him why there had to be so much pain in our lives. I heard him responding, "Because there is pain in God, too." I had never thought of God as suffering; wasn't he omnipotent? True, I had always known Jesus, the Son of God, endured suffering. But with this new insight, something shifted inside me as I heard again the desolate cry of Jesus in the garden, begging his Father to take away the cup of his anguish. At that moment I realized that this was a cry of the Cosmic Christ. Only Jesus could cry out with this intensity, because only he was the link between God and the universe, having perfect understanding of everything created on this side of heaven. He accepted what his Father asked, and so his cry became the cry that leads to our rebirthing in paradise.

It became so clear to me that suffering has a transcendent dimension; if we see our suffering as Jesus' suffering, then we are one with him in rebirthing our world. With this vision, suffering ceases to block our breathing and growing. We become the new humanity, shaped by the teachings of Jesus. We become as he was, a child of God, compassionate and loving to others.

I am comforted in my suffering because in my Lenten journey with Jesus I have learned that, truly, we are never alone. Long ago Isaiah prophesied (53:1–12) that one would come to bear "the sins of many" in death and open the door for us to the Father's realm. Some believe this passage refers to the atoning death of a suffering individual, and others believe it refers to the Jewish people, a "suffering group." Reflecting on suffering and hope in *Jesus and the Holocaust,* author Joel Marcus offers an interpretation worth considering. He suggests that Isaiah 53:1-12 "is testimony to the amazing power of Jesus to break through human misunderstanding and to present himself anew, unshackled from human preconceptions, to each generation."

In the chapters that follow, I hope to underscore my own insights about "the amazing power of Jesus." In his public life, beginning with his Lent—his temptation in the desert—and ending in his going from the tomb to the light of resurrection, we are given assurance that when we face the smorgasbord of life, with its offerings of confusion, pain, laughter, sorrow, hope, fear, and so much more, we are not alone because we hold Jesus' hand. He has pioneered the path to show us our Father's faithful love, which may often be blurred in desert haze, but is, in fact, a permanent gift for each of us...the gift of eternal life.

Prayer

From Isaiah 53

Who has believed what we have heard?
    And to whom has the arm of the LORD been
        revealed?
For he grew up before him like a young plant,
    and like a root out of dry ground;
he had no form or majesty that we should look at him,
    nothing in his appearance that we should desire him.
He was despised and rejected by others;
    a man of suffering and acquainted with infirmity;
and as one from whom others hide their faces
    he was despised, and we held him of no account.

Surely he has borne our infirmities
    and carried our diseases;
yet we accounted him stricken,
    struck down by God, and afflicted.
But he was wounded for our transgressions,
    crushed for our iniquities;
upon him was the punishment that made us whole,
    and by his bruises we are healed.
All we like sheep have gone astray;
    we have all turned to our own way,
and the LORD has laid on him the
    iniquity of us all.

Lent: An Uncommon Love Story

He was oppressed, and he was afflicted,
>   yet he did not open his mouth;
like a lamb that is led to the slaughter,
>   and like a sheep that before its shearers is silent,
>   so he did not open his mouth.
By a perversion of justice he was taken away.
>   Who could have imagined his future?
For he was cut off from the land of the living,
>   stricken for the transgression of my people.
They made his grave with the wicked
>   and his tomb with the rich,
although he had done no violence,
>   and there was no deceit in his mouth.

Yet it was the will of the LORD to crush him with pain.
When you make his life an offering for sin,
>   he shall see his offspring, and shall prolong his
>   days;
through him the will of the LORD shall prosper.
>   Out of his anguish he shall see light;
he shall find satisfaction through his knowledge.
>   The righteous one, my servant, shall make many
>   righteous,
>   and he shall bear their iniquities.

Therefore I will allot him a portion with the great,
>   and he shall divide the spoil with the strong;

because he poured out himself to death,
    and was numbered with the transgressors;
yet he bore the sin of many,
    and made intercession for the transgressors.

2

Lent Is a Time for Reflecting on Love

"Being sad in Jesus' presence is an existential impossibility."
— *Rev. Edward Schillebeechx*

For ten years of my life, beginning at age eight, when Holy Week arrived every year, I was wedded to the liturgy and commemoration of Jesus' last days. I was privileged to live in the Cathedral parish of the city of Albany, New York, where the prayers and pageantry of Holy Week, led by the bishop, were mine to share simply by walking the few blocks from home to the Cathedral.

The solemnity of the week began with Tenebrae services early Wednesday evening. I was enthralled by the mystery I felt, inherent in the ceremony of progressively eliminating light, down to the last candle, until the church was in darkness...as was the world which put Christ—the light of the world—to death. Adding to the beauty of the services was the Franciscan monk's choir from St. Anthony-on-Hudson. Even without benefit of the organ, their blended voices were so harmonious in singing the mysterious Latin words that I truly felt I was in a place "out of this world."

For me, Holy Thursday offered the most special liturgy of the year. Until I was too old, I used to march in procession in my white dress and veil, feeling very proud of belonging to it all. The ceremony was very long, but I never felt bored or tired. While the bells rang gloriously, the choir sang the last Gloria to be heard until Holy Saturday. When they stopped, the silence, in contrast to the joyous sounds, was again effectively symbolic of a world stilled by its rejection of Christ.

On Holy Thursday evening, my father would drive us to visit the churches in the city, each with its open, empty tabernacle, and the altar beautifully decorated with satin cloths, lilies, and other white flowers. We would always visit an odd number of churches. For some reason, unknown to me, it was an Italian tradition to visit an odd—rather than even—number of churches!

On Good Friday, my older sister Rosemary and I went to the Cathedral at noon, staying a full three hours in total

Lent: An Uncommon Love Story

silence, honoring the One who loved us so much he was willing to be nailed to a cross for all that time. I didn't understand the theology at that young age, but I certainly understood that Jesus was doing this because he loved me. At 3 P.M. we always fully expected the sun to stop shining and thunder to start. (It was strange how often the sky did cloud up at that hour on Good Friday!)

During those three hours, if we became restless from kneeling and sitting, we would walk to the altar and crouch down almost to a prone position to kiss the crucifix placed on a cushion at the base of the altar rail. Or we'd pray the Stations of the Cross. The doors of the tabernacles of the Cathedral's five altars were open to show their emptiness. The sense of loss was heavy, making the meaning of Good Friday terribly real to us.

On Holy Saturday, I closely followed the before-Mass ceremonies. But all the while I impatiently waited for the Gloria, when the bells sounded loud, long, and triumphant, and the organ would be played again. The jubilation of these sounds during the Easter vigil mesmerized me, making my seduction by the Triduum liturgy complete.

Rosemary and I always went prepared to bring home some of the newly blessed holy water. We each carried a shiny, clean, glass quart milk bottle to be filled. When we entered the house after Mass, my mother took the holy water, sprinkled some on us, and then around every room of the house, asking God to bless us and our home for another year.

It is a long time since those days when I lived my introduction to the liturgical richness of Holy Week. But even now, each year I relive the passion and glory of Holy Week as I experienced it in the church I still call "my cathedral." And rooted in me since that time is the lesson I learned: the real, difficult definition of love. On the cross, Jesus set the model for what it means to truly love, and this has ever remained what we might call "hard stuff to swallow," because none of us wants to face the vulnerability that is the price tag attached to love. Certainly, none of us would ever thrill to have our love tested by his standard of "no one has greater love than this, to lay down one's life for one's friends." Yet, Jesus defined love in terms of what one is willing to give of oneself for another.

On the cross Jesus showed that he set no limits on his own love. Even in his tormenting pain, he could offer love and forgiveness to others. He asked his Father to forgive those who put him to death, for they didn't know what they were doing. For the penitent thief on a cross by his side, who asked to be remembered when Jesus went to his Father's kingdom, Jesus, profoundly moved by this declaration of love, promised "Paradise." As Julia Vitullo-Martin, a social worker for justice, once wrote: "Jesus' dying words of love and forgiveness have seldom guided humanity for long. But they are the ultimate message of Easter."

I remember this Easter message of love being expressed to me by a man who had two "near death experiences." A former Marine, Dannion Brinkley was hit by a bolt of lightning that came through a telephone line during a thunderstorm in September 1975. He was 25, and according to hospital records, he remained dead for 28 minutes. He describes being guided during this time by "a Being of light," and having "a panoramic view of my life."

He told me, "If you think everything's not 'recorded,' ha! But the *big* thing is how much love you gave others. No one judged me, but *me*," he said, and then admitted that he had not been a very nice person in his young years.

Because the lightning shock had badly weakened his heart, Dannion "died" again fourteen years later. Again, he was received by the "Being of light," but now the review of his life was very different. Dannion had radically changed, working as a hospice volunteer who was devoted to helping people. He had learned in his first "journey" that "as you give, so you receive...there is life after death...we are children of God and a part of us is that exalted spark—and *all that matters is how much love you have shown."* This is, indeed, Jesus' Easter message, delivered *in person* to all of us.

There is another love story that we perhaps overlook when we remember Jesus dying on the cross. It is that of Mary, Jesus' Mother, standing at the foot of the cross. This image haunts me: Mary must have been thinking of the joy Jesus had brought into her life and the lives of all those he met, precisely because he was a lover of all. She could probably remember his respectful handling of the wood he worked with, his smile at the birds, his reverencing the trees, and playing with children. Mary was the one who had watched him take his first steps, making sure he didn't fall, who no doubt later worried that he'd hurt himself with the sharp tools in the carpentry shop. That's what mothers are like, protectors. And yet, at the last moment, Mary couldn't save her Son.

The image of Mary holding her dead Son always touched me deeply. But it wasn't until I, too, had to confront lifeless sons that I really could identify with Mary and share her agonizing pain. I think we sometimes do Mary a disservice. We venerate the Pietà, and acknowledge Mary's sorrow at receiving the bloodied, mangled body of her Son as he was taken down from the cross. But I don't think our image of Mary is as it really was on that Good Friday. Most of us prefer to see the beautiful, youthful woman as envisioned by Michelangelo, silently holding the white marble body of her son. Not me. I hear a mother screaming in pain.

I've heard sermons suggesting that Mary knew she was the Mother of God, and although she suffered to see Jesus die on the cross, she knew he was saving the world. But I don't think Mary was given a kind of noonday vision of eternity that kept her levitating despite her pain. I think, on the contrary, that she was given the most difficult burden of all. She was to be the first Christian, the first follower, the first to be confused by the unfolding of her Son's life, the first to have to fall down on her face and acknowledge the mystery of what was happening. She surely understood that Jesus was like no other man, that he had a message of love to bring to this world. I think Mary, following the Son she had loved so much,

On the cross, Jesus set the model for what it means to truly love, and this has ever remained what we might call "hard stuff to swallow," because none of us wants to face the vulnerability that is the price tag attached to love.

had the hardest, thorniest journey of all who were there on that Friday.

I saw this so clearly in a most unusual way after my son Peter died. I had gone to England to begin religious studies at Oxford, in hopes of finding some help with my pain and confusion. One day I found a church with a side chapel. Above the altar of that chapel, filling the wall, was a three-dimensional, full-color sculpture of the Pietà. I was mesmerized by this agonized Mother, who seemed to be holding not only her Son, but every hurting person in the world—myself included.

As I cried with her, she gave me a loving gift. Suddenly I could see my Peter. He was with Jesus—and they were dancing! Mary, infused with the love of her Son, has never left us to endure our confusions and sufferings alone, and she didn't leave me alone in my time of need. Mary was there first, and she waits to reach out to all of us. Mary—in the searing reality of the Pietà—is Lent's other, enduring gift of love.

Of course, Christ is the one from whom the *greatest* love—love as never known before—radiated. E. Stanley Jones, long ago sharing stories of his personal, spiritual awakening, proclaimed:

He lived with people, and before them. And in his words, they heard the Word—the Word that he was. When he spoke of love they knew what it meant, for they had seen it—had seen it in his face, his deeds, in him. When he spoke of God they felt his presence, for he came, not proclaiming God; he brought him....

Here was One who showed by word and by work, by trial and by triumph, by smiting and by smile, by goodness and by service what the Heart of the universe is like.

I truly believe that Jesus, in his Lenten desert, was shown by his Father what love could do if only the people of the world, then and now, could hear and accept its meaning. When Jesus said "yes" to his Father, the life he went on to live became the love story that redeemed the world. As poet Edwin Markham once wrote:

Here is the Truth in a little creed,
Enough for all the roads we go:
In Love is all the law we need,
In Christ is all the God we know.

Lent: An Uncommon Love Story

Back in the '80s, when I was the editor of a Connecticut newspaper, I got a call from a local Kmart store telling me that this national retail chain was offering a program to provide Easter holiday meals for needy families. I was surprised and positively impressed; while I knew of some commercial enterprises reaching out to give gifts to the poor at Thanksgiving and Christmas, I hadn't heard of any Easter gifts.

In my news story on this Easter program, I quoted the then-company chairman of the retail corporation, who said it was intended "to show concern for the 35.3 million persons who live in poverty in our country," a number which, sadly, has remained about the same some twenty years later.

Because this kindness was expressed at Easter time, it reminded me that the compassion we find in this world is truly rooted in the teachings, the life, the death, and the resurrection of Jesus. His was a firm message of how we should help and care for one another: "I was hungry and you gave me food." "When, Lord, when?" "Just as you did it to one of the least of these who are members of my family, you did it to me" (cf. Mt 23:35–40). Could his urging that we love one another, continuing and carrying out his example, have been any clearer?

So many, united to us in the Communion of Saints, have heard and embraced this message to love one another, the same message that Jesus never wavered from during his lifetime. I learned about one of these extraordinary persons through my late son Sterling, who was a Fourth Degree Knight of Columbus, and told me proudly of the Knight's founder, Father Michael J. McGivney, whose cause for canonization has been introduced.

Born August 12, 1852, Michael was the oldest of thirteen children, six of whom died before reaching adolescence. His parents were immigrants who had fled the potato famine in Ireland and settled in Waterbury, Connecticut, the home of brass mills, where they knew deep poverty. To help his parents put food on the table, Michael left school at thirteen to work in a spoon-making factory. When he was nineteen, his father died.

A local priest, who saw an unusual potential in this young man, arranged to help him get an education. Michael eventually knew he wanted to be a priest and he was ordained in 1877. His first assignment was St. Mary's in New Haven, and the people he served were mainly Polish, Italian, and Irish immigrants, who worked in the mills and were disparaged by their well-off, established neighbors.

Lent: An Uncommon Love Story

Knowing the pain of severe poverty, and of burying overworked fathers who died too young, this caring priest began to organize laymen in his parish to find a way to help the widows and orphans he continually encountered. From this effort the Knights of Columbus was born, a group that developed practical ways to ensure assistance to working families should the bread-winner die in a factory accident or of fatigue, as Father McGivney's own father had died.

The stress of factory work at a young age and the effects of having suffered, because of poverty, childhood diseases, along with years of overwork for families and children, left Father McGivney particularly vulnerable to illness. He died on August 14, 1890, at the age of thirty-eight, but his legacy of compassion goes on in the good work still being done by the group he founded.

I have met so many people who, like Father McGivney, have walked in Jesus' footsteps, understanding that he is calling us to a life centered in God, and that he came to show us who God is if we but journey with him. Jesus wants us to be like him—to have reverence for food, love for the birds and the trees, joyful playtime with children, forgiveness of those who trespass against us, and love for our neighbors. He was so fully human that he would undergo physical death, trusting his Father's promise that this would not be an ending, but a beginning that would transform the world. What greater love has ever been present in this world since the dawn of creation? What better time is there to reflect on this love than Lent?

God gives us "steadfast love..."—this is the proclamation of Psalm 89:

> *I will sing of your steadfast love, O Lord,*
> > *forever;*
> > *with my mouth I will proclaim your faithfulness*
> > *to all generations.*
> *I declare that your steadfast love is established*
> > *forever;*
> > *your faithfulness is as firm as the heavens*
> > *(vv. 1–2).*

Theologian Richard F. Vieth, reflecting on this promise, links its permanence to Jesus:

> The New Testament extends this understanding of God and gives it its own unique turn.... The "steadfast love" of God lauded by the psalmist is reflected in the New Testament's paeans to God's love, culminating in John's bold claim that "God is love" (1 Jn 4:8).

Lent: An Uncommon Love Story

Prayer

From Psalm 89:1–9, 47–52

I will sing of your steadfast love, O L ORD, forever;
    with my mouth I will proclaim your faithfulness to
        all generations.
I declare that your steadfast love is established forever;
    your faithfulness is as firm as the heavens.

You said, "I have made a covenant with my
        chosen one,
    I have sworn to my servant David:
'I will establish your descendants forever,
    and build your throne for all generations.'"

Let the heavens praise your wonders, O L ORD,
    your faithfulness in the assembly of the holy ones.
For who in the skies can be compared to the L ORD?
    Who among the heavenly beings is like the L ORD,
a God feared in the council of the holy ones,
    great and awesome above all that are around him?
O L ORD God of hosts,
    who is as mighty as you, O L ORD?
    Your faithfulness surrounds you.
You rule the raging of the sea;
    when its waves rise, you still them.

Remember how short my time is—
    for what vanity you have created all mortals!
Who can live and never see death?
    Who can escape the power of Sheol?

Lord, where is your steadfast love of old,
    which by your faithfulness you swore to David?
Remember, O LORD, how your servant is taunted;
    how I bear in my bosom the insults of the peoples,
with which your enemies taunt, O LORD,
    with which they taunted the footsteps of your
        anointed.

Blessed be the LORD forever. Amen and Amen.

Jesus, in his Lenten desert, was
shown by his Father what love
could do if only the people of
the world, then and now, could
hear and accept its meaning.
When Jesus said "yes" to his
Father, the life he went on to
live became the love story that
redeemed the world.

3

Lent Is the Promise That Love Will Conquer Despair

"I will exult and rejoice in your steadfast love,
because you have seen my affliction;
you have taken heed of my adversities..."
— Psalm 31:7

Lent is a kind of "moment of truth" in a Christian's life. It deals with the basic need we will all one day face: how to hang on to faith when we're in the desert. I learned that during a hard, hard period of my life when I was a single parent, trying to heal from a disastrous marriage, raise and support six children with only the help they themselves could give me. At that time I used to say to myself, *I'm in the season of Lent—the long, dark days in the desert.* I wanted release from the pain of worrying whether I was being a good parent and giving my children the right example of how to live with trust in the

Lord, and from the pain of the personal loneliness in my life, the sad lot of any parent who has lost a partner from death or abandonment.

I found myself on my knees late at night, often close to despair from the fatigue of working 18-hour days. Sometimes I quietly screamed at God inside my head, angry that he wasn't the "fix-it" God I had envisioned in my younger days. But soon enough, I began to suspect I wasn't alone. I started feeling like I was in the desert with Jesus, being tested, as he was, on the choices I would make in those dark days—choices that would determine who I would become as my life went on. There, with Jesus, I found the strength to sustain me. And it did, even when, a few years later, life brought me the crucifying blows of losing two sons. With my focus on this desert time, I began to analyze what Lent was really about— and *that* was the beginning of my healing.

After Jesus' resurrection, the early Church observed days of fasting prior to the Easter celebration. Gradually, underscoring the days of Jesus' fasting in the desert, this period was lengthened from just a few days to forty, and eventually it was called "Lent," a mid-English term for "springtime." My own darkness took me back to that desert experience, when "Lent" was inevitable in the life of our Lord Jesus.

There, I came to understand that the carpenter's son knew he would be attacked and persecuted when he went public with his new message—that he had come to show people that his Father's world was never meant to be one of selfishness and violence, but rather a world that emphasized love above all. He would make quite a stir, bringing on many enemies. He knew he could be apprehended and that, should he face pain and death, because he was fully human he would lose the brightness of the noonday sun. His mission would become blurry in the ensuing gloom. He would reach the pit where he would feel betrayed and abandoned by his Father.

Out of his need to prepare for the darkness of near despair, Jesus retreated to the desert to wrestle with his doubts, to recharge his trust in the Father, to solidify his determination to see his hard mission through. He needed this time to build up his strength so as not to waver, come failure, betrayal, and cross.

In the desert, Jesus spent forty days building up his trust in his Father, gaining the courage to face what was coming. In those forty days, I believe Jesus was united with every person ever given life—and that he felt their tragedies, their emptiness, their despair. As he was tempted by Satan in his worn-down condition, I believe that he saw how the seduction of evil would be the permanent enemy working to destroy his Father's world. He must have seen what hatred can do and felt the torment of future killings, wars, murders, and the abuses that would be piled by humans upon other humans. He must have felt in his soul the tragedies of nature, where earthquakes, storms, volcanoes, illness, and other calamities would periodically strike defenseless humans.

Jesus must have come close to despair in the desert. Yet, I believe in the end he felt such love for every child of his Father, everyone born since the dawn of creation, that he was willing to see his mission through, even though it meant he would have to die for each one of us. Why? Jesus' death proved that earthly death is not the end of our existence, but a transition to a new life too glorious to be understood or even imagined on this earth.

In the desert Jesus spent forty days building up trust in the Father and gaining the courage to face what was coming, even though, humanly, he did not know for sure

Lent: An Uncommon Love Story

that there was a road out of the desert, or an Easter after the execution.

That was the first Lent, and it was, truly, a love story.

When the early Christians decided that Lent would be built into the liturgical year leading to Easter—determining that this would be the proper time for catechumens to prepare for baptism—it *had* to be related to that love story. It had to spring from the honest admission that, like our Founder, all Christians would be plagued by the vagaries of faith, a faith that can seem as comforting as a security blanket one minute and as tormenting as a fickle lover the next.

I've often thought that the term "gift of faith" can be confusing. We might assume that, as with the gift of baptism, faith is something "automatic," and that once we have it, we can "lose it" only by the most perverse self-willing. In truth, despite its power and grace, the way we humanly respond to the gift of faith can be affected by what is happening in our lives. When life is pleasant, faith is an easy part of the package. But life can bring the death

All of us experience the desert,
and it is in the desert that we can
rediscover trust in Jesus' love. We
can reaffirm fidelity to him so as
not to break down under the
blackness of the Good Friday
cross. Lent, as well as Easter,
is our heritage.

of a child, the divorce of parents, a grown child turned selfish and ugly, a debilitating disease, a desperate internal boredom, an untouchable loneliness, confinement to a home for the aged. Can many of us honestly say that our faith feels so strong that we are certain of facing terrifying events with complete conviction that God is still with us?

I myself walk the tightrope between yes and no when it comes to faith. The early deaths of two beloved sons severely stretched that tightrope, bringing me close to the breaking point. But I haven't fallen off yet. When my Lents return—like now, as I face the recent loss of my son, Sterling, and the unknown future of my younger brother, Joseph, who is suffering from pancreatic cancer—I go back with Jesus for those forty days of searching. I feel scared stiff before the crosses "lying in wait" for me, yet I also take courage from the remembrance that Jesus himself wasn't handed faith on a silver platter. Jesus was spared neither suffering nor the cross. If he could go on to face Good Friday, not really knowing with certainty there would be an Easter, can't I hang on? Can't I go on believing that no matter where I stand in the darkness, it is still within the inner circle of God's arms? That's when I go back to the desert to reflect again on the decision of our Lord Jesus to love us to the death—and despair loses its hold on me.

My faith convinces me that Lent is the promise, never to be denied, that our true gift is love, straight from the Father, and that this love is stronger than all pain and evil evident in this world. In a book called "The Jesus Myth," written some four decades ago, author Father Andrew Greeley affirms this love:

> There was not the slightest hint of cheap consolation in Jesus' message. He did not deny the reality of suffering or death. He simply asserted that God was love and that love triumphed in the end. He did not say that injustice was to be quietly accepted. He did not say that suffering was to be overlooked or that pain was to be denied. Rather, he addressed himself to something much more elemental and asserted that, despite suffering, despite injustice, despite misery, and despite death, everything would still be all right in the end. Because His Father was love...

Because of my personal experience of bereavement, I know extreme pain. Subsequently, I have done a lot of work with hurting people. I hope to share with them what I have learned from pain—that, if we don't stay stuck in the darkness of the desert, pain can give us a new and valuable blueprint for living that we could never have imagined.

Not long ago a woman, suffering from the sudden death of a small child, challenged me for what she called my "optimism." She said she had lost her faith, and justified this by saying she believed Jesus had also given up on God as he suffered on the cross. She referred over and over to his lament, when he said, "My God, my God, why have you forsaken me?" She asked, "Where was God's answer?" And, since God did not respond to Jesus' cry, she insisted that he had died in despair.

That wasn't the first time I had heard people struggle with those words. I myself had sometimes repeated them in the despairing moments of my life. Because those words so burned in my soul, and seemed to be a cry of despair, I desperately sought to understand what was really going on in Jesus' mind when he uttered that wrenching lament. And one day, I had the good fortune to learn what Jesus meant.

When I had taken courses in Religious Studies at Oxford a few years back, I had N. T. Wright, a noted New Testament scholar, as one of my teachers. Dr. Wright, now the Canon theologian at Westminster Abbey in England, pointed out that those words of Jesus—"My God, my God, why have you forsaken me?"—are often misinterpreted as being a sign of despair. They are the first sentence of Psalm 22, and, although the Psalm begins with this cry, it ends with an affirmation not only of hope but also of the coming of the kingdom of the Lord. It was an eye-opener for me.

This Psalm should be read often, certainly during Lent. The words of the first part can move us to tears:

> *Why are you so far from helping me, from the*
> *words of my groaning?*
> *...I am a worm, and not human;*
> *scorned by others, and despised by the*
> *people.*
> *All who see me mock at me;*
> *they make mouths at me, they shake their*
> *heads;*
> *"Commit your cause to the LORD; let him*
> *deliver—*
> *let him rescue the one in whom he delights!"*

Lent: An Uncommon Love Story

And then follows the sheer poetry of this affirmation:

Yet it was you who took me from the womb;
 you kept me safe on my mother's breast.
On you I was cast from my birth,
 and since my mother bore me you have been
  my God" (Ps 22:1, 6–10).

The Psalm swells in acknowledging the goodness of God, and ends with a prophecy of how God's goodness will be made known to all future generations.

One thing we know is that Jesus was a teacher. He certainly knew the Old Testament, as it were, "by chapter and verse." When he spoke the first words of Psalm 22, he knew what he was doing. He was not disclosing despair, but rather, the opposite. We've often heard only the "forsaken" words and not the rest of the Psalm that he must have been whispering to himself, repeating it in his heart as he was dying in torment, and trusting in the Father for all that would come.

Certainly what would come would be astounding. For it would be by Jesus' life—transformed and remaining ever in this world, beginning that first Easter morn— that the Lord would always be made known, that all of life on earth would forever come from a love story rooted in eternity.

I think the words of South African Bishop Desmond Tutu are another affirmation of the great Psalm 22: "Easter means that hope prevails over despair.... Easter says to us that despite everything to the contrary, his will [and love] for us will prevail...." Certainly, that was the truth Jesus wanted us to grasp. Easter is the victory over all darkness.

And Lent is the pathway, a love story that holds a wondrous promise fulfilled on Easter morning.

Prayer

From Psalm 22:1–11, 27–31

My God, my God, why have you forsaken me?
    Why are you so far from helping me, from the
        words of my groaning?
O my God, I cry by day, but you do not answer;
    and by night, but find no rest.

Yet you are holy,
    enthroned on the praises of Israel.
In you our ancestors trusted;
    they trusted, and you delivered them.
To you they cried, and were saved;
    in you they trusted, and were not put to shame.

Lent: An Uncommon Love Story

But I am a worm, and not human;
    scorned by others, and despised by
        the people.
All who see me mock at me;
    they make mouths at me, they shake their heads;
"Commit your cause to the LORD; let him deliver—
    let him rescue the one in whom he delights!"

Yet it was you who took me from the womb;
    you kept me safe on my mother's breast.
On you I was cast from my birth,
    and since my mother bore me you have been
        my God.
Do not be far from me,
    for trouble is near
        and there is no one to help.

All the ends of the earth shall remember
    and turn to the LORD;
and all the families of the nations
        shall worship before him.
For dominion belongs to the LORD,
    and he rules over the nations.

To him, indeed, shall all who sleep in the earth bow
        down;
    before him shall bow all who go down to the dust,
    and I shall live for him.

Posterity will serve him;
    future generations will be told about the LORD,
and proclaim his deliverance to a people yet unborn,
    saying that he has done it.

4

How Lent Brings Us Back to Reality

"I would not want human wisdom and eloquence to intervene in my poor speech, because then I would be giving you the world's vanity and not the wisdom of the Crucified."

— *Archbishop Oscar Romero*

Several years ago a Catholic university program director asked me if I would present a talk on "Finding Meaning in Everyday Life." I thought the topic would be a piece of cake until I started working on what I'd say. So much comes to mind when we begin thinking of our everyday routine—getting up on time, making breakfast, getting the children off to school or yourself off to work. But everyday life is also about the unexpected, like the car breaking down, the alarming phone call telling you a family member is ill, tripping on a rug and taking a bad fall, finding out that a good friend has had a stroke.

I soon realized that this was a very difficult topic, actually even a painful one. In order to find meaning in the daily events of our lives, not only do we have to consider the mundane, but we must also wrestle with the life-shattering. In my life, I had already discovered that there is only one way to find meaning in everything we do and experience: finding God in all of it. And for me, there's only one way to see God in all the minutes of our life. We need faith: a trust that we can accept even though it brings no answers to why life happens the way it does.

Rather than answers, faith brings us something better. In a word, Jesus, and his "blueprint" for how to live our everyday lives, found on every page of the Gospels. If we do "put on Christ," as Saint Paul encourages, then everyday life, from the mundane to the spectacular to the cross, has meaning. Then we become immersed in the reality we were meant to have as our earthly milieu—love-drenched days sanctified by the breath of God.

Admittedly, to think or speak this way does not place one in a very popular position, as so well demonstrated in the lives of saints and martyrs such as Archbishop Oscar Romero of El Salvador. He was murdered on March 24, 1980, by men who held worldly power. These, his countrymen, hated him both because of his words and his work to help his desperately poor and suffering people. Romero knew that the realities that had shaped his life—his choice to remain faithful to God's justice and the Gospel of Jesus Christ—put his life in danger. Yet he accepted this danger, saying:

> We should not wonder that the Church has a lot of cross to bear. Otherwise, it will not have a lot of resurrection. An accommodating Church, a Church that seeks prestige without the pain of the cross, is not the authentic Church of Jesus Christ.

If there is one thing that we learn from the lives of Christ-followers like Oscar Romero, it is the importance of learning and staying with what is really important in life. This is what Jesus consistently tried to help us understand. Yes, it is important to work, to create our housing, to feed and clothe ourselves and our children, to learn, to try to maintain good health, to refrain from polluting the air, earth, and seas. All of this emerges from the words of our Lord Jesus Christ, found in the Gospels, but something else comes across, too. In modern terminology, we could call it the admonition, "Don't sweat the small stuff. Stick with what really matters." In our personal lives, don't we too often spend chunks of our days making mountains out of temporary molehills? I hate to think of how much energy I wasted in my younger years worrying about whether the turkey was moist enough, if I had gained two pounds, if this dress was appropriate for the occasion, or if I said the right thing at that dinner get-together.

Who remembers what we wore or ate three days ago? Yet, we can so easily waste our precious lives worrying about petty details and petty conflicts rather than seeking enduring truths. My sister called me one day to find out how things were going with a problem that I had spent time venting about during a long distance phone call a week earlier. I was embarrassed to admit I couldn't remember what it was!

We get upset and rattled over fleeting problems at work, arguments with family and/or neighbors, or even the leak in the dishwasher or the broken lawn mower. We so often allow ourselves to be overwhelmed with day-to-day difficulties, which take too much of our attention and energy if we don't keep things in perspective. And in most cases, the small things we label "problems" soon fade into oblivion!

Lent: An Uncommon Love Story

If we're honest with ourselves, it's no mystery why we put so much time and energy into our temporary problems. It's because we are always trying to get control over our lives. In our hearts, we know that real control is impossible; the specter of some sudden natural or man-made disaster always looms over our heads. But until we give up that futile struggle to "have it my way," we won't find true peace. It is only a "loose grasp on life," with a sense of surrender to God's will, that can bring lasting freedom and fulfillment. Even for psychological good health, we are better off with an attitude of patience for the long term than of control over the moment.

When we get mired down in issues that soon fade, we can lose sight of Jesus' teaching about what is eternally important: his Father's loving plan, not what's going on in the town council, or the PTA, or the Monday morning meeting. Although these events are necessary, we need to constantly remind ourselves that the cities, towns, jobs, and houses we inhabit here on earth are not our lasting home.

Lent, which brings us back to the desert, is the clearest reminder we have that all things are passing except for the truth that Jesus so clearly defined when he said,

If we do "put on Christ," as Saint
Paul encourages, then everyday
life, from the mundane to the
spectacular to the cross, has
meaning. Then we become
immersed in the reality we were
meant to have as our earthly
milieu—love-drenched days
sanctified by the breath of God.

"Father, thy word is truth." This is more than a proclamation by Jesus. It is a call to understand what is most important—our Father's enduring presence defining the very minutes of our lives. Mohandas K. Gandhi expressed it thus:

> It is better to allow our lives to speak for us than our words. God did not bear the cross only two thousand years ago. He bears it today, and he dies and is resurrected from day to day. It would be a poor comfort to the world if it had to depend on a historical God who died two thousand years ago. Do not, then, preach the God of history, but show him as he lives today through you.

Our Catholic bishops have also kept alive the Lord's word in extraordinary documents that speak to the current and emerging problems of our world. Notable is their pastoral letter on war and peace, issued several months before the dawn of Easter 1984, dealing with the nuclear arms build-up that had become our worst enemy, putting the existence of life as we know it in jeopardy.

In that letter, the bishops linked the message of Easter with the need to face the nuclear arms reality. They emphasized: "It is our belief in the risen Christ which sustains us in confronting the awesome challenge of the nuclear arms race." They alluded to the Easter event, saying: "Jesus Christ...is our peace and in his death-resurrection, he gives God's peace to our world.... The risen Lord's gift of peace is inextricably bound to the call to follow Jesus and to continue the proclamation of God's reign."

The image of "breaking out," emerging from the empty tomb, surrounds Easter. (Even commercially, think of chicks breaking out of eggs and lilies bursting open.) But the bishops' words underscored how we now have created a dark side of "breaking out" through weapons. If the destruction inside a nuclear warhead breaks out, wholesale death will be our destiny. We will have turned the order of God's world into a chaos wrecking human life. "We are the first generation since Genesis with the power to virtually destroy God's creation," the bishops said, pointing to the horror of a nuclear war, which would make the world a wasteland incapable of supporting life, the ultimate "no" to God, the climactic mortal sin.

Poet Stanton A. Coblentz asked the question that arose after the twentieth century's two World Wars that is ever more piercing today:

What would he say should he come once more,
And saw a shuddering planet burn and bleed...
As though in a dream, I hear a soul-deep plea
That throbs and murmurs from a measureless source,
I view a figure preaching; and I see
The crowds that form in raillery or remorse.
And then I mark a crimsoned, nail-pierced tree,
And a torn sufferer moaning on a cross.

It is always a struggle to keep our focus on the will of God before taking on man-made concerns. Nothing is harder than putting compassion above self-centeredness, and Gospel values above material pursuits and status-seeking. Ultimately, however, at the end of our physical lives, only the issues that are intimately linked with God and his yearnings for us will stand before us. In the long run, the only questions will be whether we joined Jesus in truly accepting our God-ordered responsibility to love others, whether we rose to the challenges of our God-given faith, and how much we connected to our real, eternal home during our temporary stay on earth.

Lent brings us back to reality because of the lessons we relearn in its forty days. There in the desert with Jesus, we are reminded that in spite of how hard we try to keep our lives ordered and comfortable, most of us don't reach our expectations. Life brings its own agenda: illness, family troubles, weather disasters, accidents, marriage break-ups, and, yes, death of loved ones. We aren't in charge of what happens to us in life, only how we handle it.

We all run the risk of locking into routines that make us comfortable, that make us feel as if we are, indeed, in charge of our lives. We seek to control our very minutes, even if only in matters that are relatively unimportant. When my mother reached her mid-80s, I would call her only to be told that she couldn't talk because this was the time she had a snack, or made her tea, or took a walk, or watched a particular television program.

If we can stay focused on Jesus in the desert, we can learn to trust the Father more, believing that every time we pray for bread and we receive something that looks more like a pickle, or a stone, or a crown of thorns, we should be patient and look again. For it is really *bread*. We simply don't recognize it as bread, because it doesn't fit our image of what we need for the moment's nourishment.

I read a very good book, *Stupid Ways, Smart Ways to Think About God,* by Rabbi Jack Bemporad and author Michael Shevack. They point out how God cannot be fashioned in our image, cannot be shaped by the hands of time or our hands, because, "God never simmered in the cosmic Crock Pot that gave birth to the universe. He was the cook." And, I add, that like all good cooks, God kept some of his recipes secret (and that includes some of his bread recipes!).

Jesus himself was seeking "bread" when he prayed in the Garden of Olives, asking his Father to take away the coming chalice of pain and death. He didn't get what he asked for, but trusted what his Father had in store for him. And the Father asked his Son to give unconditional love to all, so that all people would learn to give unconditional love to others. From this, Jesus gave us a new commandment: "Love one another, as I have loved you."

Viktor Frankl, a survivor of a long imprisonment in a Nazi concentration camp, expressed the power of love that he was given to understand even as he suffered:

A thought transfixed me; for the first time in my life I saw the truth as it is set into song by so many poets, proclaimed as the final wisdom by so many thinkers. The truth—that love is the ultimate and the highest goal to which man can aspire. Then I grasped the meaning of the greatest secret that human poetry and human thought and belief has to impart: the salvation of man is *through* love and *in* love.... For the first time in my life, I was able to understand the meaning of the words, "The angels are lost in perpetual contemplation of an infinite glory."

Jesus lived and died to teach us how to discern what is important in life and what we were created to do. Bottom line? Hear the Father's word, as the Son spoke it, lived it, and died for it, and know *this* is the truth. Grasp this, and no matter what pain or evil exists, we can know joy.

Lent: An Uncommon Love Story

Prayer

From 1 Peter 2:21–24

...Christ also suffered for you, leaving you an example, so that you should follow in his steps.

"He committed no sin,
>   and no deceit was found in his mouth."

When he was abused, he did not return abuse; when he suffered, he did not threaten; but he entrusted himself to the one who judges justly. He himself bore our sins in his body on the cross, so that, free from sins, we might live for righteousness; by his wounds you have been healed.

5

Preparing for the Joy of Easter

"Happiness is a sort of atmosphere you can live in sometimes when you're lucky. Joy is a light that fills you with hope and faith and love."
— *Adela Rogers St. Johns*

Before Lent one year, a priest friend, giving a talk, raised an issue that struck a chord in me. He said, "Almost before we realize that Christmas is over, the priest puts on purple vestments and it is Ash Wednesday again. Last week we exulted, 'Let all the earth worship you, O Lord.' Next week we'll groan, 'The terrors of death surged around me.' Obviously, we are being reminded that a different time is about to begin.

"Then what are we being asked to do? Are we suddenly supposed to dwell on death, and the judgment of our lives and become frightened and gloomy? Certainly we are supposed to look at our lives, but we are never asked to serve the Lord in the spirit of servile fear. 'Peace' is always the word Christ greets us with. So why the change? What is this the time *for?*"

With that question decades ago, my friend put me on a personal quest to seek my own honest answer about Lent's meaning. When I was very young, I thought Lent was a time to chalk up sacrifices so I could get good marks in heaven, like grades on a report card. Lent for the young me was colored purple and fringed in black, looking something like the dresses and shawls worn to funerals by my parents' Italian women friends. Even as I got a bit older, I thought Lent was solely a time to think about my mortality, my "destiny of ashes." The result of these Lents was to put a focus on me—*my* soul and *my* salvation.

I was well into my adulthood before I discovered that, really, I had misinterpreted the road signs from Ash Wednesday to Easter. For me, Lent wasn't meant to be deep purple; it was better viewed as green, teeming with life. It wasn't all suffering and death; more profoundly, it was love and hope—all because of a spectacular ending on an earth-shaking Sunday, an ending that was a new beginning, everlasting, for everyone, until the end of earth's days.

Lent: An Uncommon Love Story

Getting to that understanding required a substantial adjustment in my thinking. In my mind, Christmas, not Lent, spoke of love. The coming of God as an innocent baby was a perfect match for love-thoughts. Knowing that the baby who had come was the one who would jolt us into a new and joyful way of interpreting human life only added to the excitement. Christmas was the promise that Jesus would transform the world with his love, and for me it was all peaches and cream.

Then came Lent, with its penitential tears, and I found it hard to remember that this, too, was a love story. It was, in fact, THE love story of all time, for it set the model for what it means to truly love. Jesus defined love in terms of what he was willing to give for another. And on that heart-wrenching Good Friday, he showed us that he set no limits on his love by fulfilling what he had told his followers: "No one has greater love than this, to lay down one's life for one's friends" (Jn 15:13). The promise of his birth was now realized. Without Good Friday, Christmas would have been just another day on which another child had been born—quite unnoticed by history. Instead, because the child of Bethlehem accepted his death on Good Friday, and rose on Easter Sunday, having proclaimed, "for this was I born," Christmas and Easter became evermore the most earth-shaking events of human history.

Remarkably, the gift Jesus wanted to pass on to us, inseparable from his love, was his joy. We should ever-remember what Jesus said to his disciples, words that we also can believe and cherish, just before he went out to be crucified. In these few words, Jesus expressed what his teachings, his "commandments," were all about. "I have said these things to you so that my joy may be in you, and that your joy may be complete. This is my commandment, that you love one another as I have loved you" (Jn 15:11–12). Jesus, an innocent man, had just been betrayed when he spoke these words; in a few hours he would be mercilessly and cruelly put to death. Yet, despite this, he was talking about joy! (As British writer C. S. Lewis would later understand, "Joy is the serious business of heaven.")

This was the legacy Jesus gave the world, but it took Good Friday to prove it. He freely accepted the darkness of personal suffering to prove to us that we, whom suffering also does not spare, are never in isolation. We do not suffer alone. Jesus suffers with us, even as he promis-

In these few words, Jesus expressed what his teachings, his "commandments," were all about. "I have said these things to you so that my joy may be in you, and that your joy may be complete. This is my commandment, that you love one another as I have loved you."

es that from his pain—from our pain—great joy awaits us. What could be more joyful than to be promised the Easter Son-rise, as proof that death is a beginning, not an end.

Since that first Easter so many of Jesus' followers and respectful admirers have radiated his joy even as they suffered severe losses. Encountering these "other Christs" amazes us! I can never forget two such examples, who never met, but who were both victims of Nazi Germany in World War II. They were innocent, yet put to death by official hate. Both Etty Hillesum and Alfred Delp had been executed during the Nazi purge—one for the "crime" of being Jewish, one for being a Catholic priest.

I used to think it was really impossible to be *in* the crucible and still able to speak of joy. Yet, the lives and deaths of Alfred Delp and Etty Hillesum left me astounded at how the human spirit, refusing to be broken, can transcend earthly crime, faithfully bearing witness to the legacy of joy inherited from the Creator.

Etty, an educated, twentieth-century woman living in Amsterdam, was caught in the menacing environment of war when the Nazis invaded Holland. She kept a diary, which was much later published as *An Interrupted Life*. I was moved to read in the introduction that as Etty was

Lent: An Uncommon Love Story

being transported by train to Auschwitz, she threw a postcard out the window. It was later found by farmers. She had written, "We have left the camp singing."

She was singing as she went to her death at age twenty-nine, on November 30, 1943, reminding me of Jesus, who spoke of joy as he went to his execution. In her diaries, Etty wrote:

> If I have one duty in these times, it is to bear witness....
> The earth is in me, and the sky...I am going to read
> St. Augustine again. He is...so full of simple devotion
> in his love letters to God. Truly, those are the only love
> letters one ought to write: love letters to God....

Father Delp was executed at age thirty-seven by the Nazis on February 2, 1945. His *Prison Writings* seem pulled from his soul and contain a truth and wisdom that perhaps can only be so strikingly expressed by someone trapped by a profound injustice. He was convicted of participating in anti-Nazi discussions. "The actual reason for my condemnation is that I happened to be and choose to remain a Jesuit," he wrote. As a follower of Christ, he also helped many Jewish people escape the Holocaust. After receiving the verdict of death, he wrote, "I was sacrificed, not conquered."

I was mesmerized as I contemplated how someone, tormented in a prison, could write: "Yet it does happen, even under these circumstances, that every now and then my whole being is flooded with pulsating life and my heart can scarcely contain the delirious joy there is in it." Like Jesus, Father Delp could speak of joy!

How much we can learn from such courageous people who manage to stay so "linked" to God. We need people like Etty, who, cold and hungry, could choose joy, writing, "I shall simply lie down and try to be a prayer." By allowing her life to become "an uninterrupted dialogue with you, O God, one great dialogue," she shared the richness and beauty God had given her.

Good Friday began the process that blasted open the tomb; Easter Sunday made us "alleluia people" capable of rejoicing and singing despite the darkness, because we're permanently celebrating such good news. Some twenty years ago, Cal Samra brought that sense of celebration to daily life. After reaching a time of near despair, Cal rediscovered the Easter that followed his personal Good Friday. His awakening led him to believe that while we should be serious about God, religion, and faith, we are often...well...*too* serious.

Lent: An Uncommon Love Story

Cal became an activist for getting people to *celebrate* the Good News of the resurrection by starting a "Fellowship of Merry Christians." In describing this needed Fellowship, he repeated a story about an Easter sermon given by the "golden-tongued" preacher, St. John Chrysostom, in which he described a vision of Christ confronting and laughing at the devil. Clearly, Cal said, God played an everlasting joke on Satan by raising Jesus from the dead. Easter deserves our joyful laughter.

That's the message Cal Samra puts yearly into his newsletter, brilliantly entitled, "The Joyful Noiseletter." "If you really believe you are saved and are going to go to heaven, for God's sake, smile!" he says. I think his wise words are worth remembering: "The cross is foolishness for those who do not believe; it is salvation, hope, and joy to those who do. It is a divine joke on Satan, the great deceiver. The empty tomb triumphs with laughter over the empty cross."

After the tragic deaths of two sons just two years apart from each other, I often thought, *I'll never be happy again.*

But then, in going through boxes of memories, I rediscovered some notes I had written inspired by a banner bought when my children were little. Hanging on the kitchen wall, it read, "Joy is the sign of God in you." That, in turn, stirred memories of the wonderful gift I had in being the mother of seven children, and I knew in my heart that while the feeling of *happiness* might elude me, I would always know *joy.* My motherhood had linked me to something bigger than myself, to the very creativity of the universe.

After this, I returned to the Gospel of John to read again how Jesus wanted to give us his *joy,* and it struck me how often we confuse joy with happiness. I could see how being happy and having fun were very good things, but these are rooted things that end in the here and now. Happiness is all tied up with time. That's why it's not enduring; we're happy one day and miserable the next. Happiness is "earthy" and therefore transitory. It is often followed by uneasiness and worry: How long will it last? When will the spell be broken?

I had believed without doubt that even though my boys had passed from this earth, they were still vibrantly alive in the hearts of those of us who loved them and in their new home in heaven. Now I could honestly say that

I was focused on the joy they had brought to our lives and on the joy I believed they now knew with their Heavenly Father. I understood Jesus' joy as never before. I knew that this joy comes from our wonderful connection with the eternal, creative, and loving Spirit of this universe.

I also understood Good Friday as never before, seeing that no matter what happens to us, no matter how many losses hit us, no matter how broken we feel, how mired in grief we become, we are the inheritors of Jesus' Easter joy—a joy that results from our connection with the Eternal, the Source of Life itself. This is the joy that makes us new people—destination heaven!

God has saturated the heavens and earth with signs of his abundant and forever Easter love. How our joy might increase if we but paid attention, as a child does. Once, a little girl was taking a walk with her father before bedtime. She kept looking up to the stars and was very quiet. Her father noticed and asked her, "What are you thinking?" She answered, with a smile, "If the bottom of heaven is so beautiful, how wonderful the other side must be."

Jesus, who had seen that "other side," lived in joy and wanted to pass his joy on to us. I believe this was the message of Christ's first miracle, done at a wedding feast, as did the well-known Russian author, Feodor Dostoevsky: "Cana of Galilee.... Ah, that sweet miracle! It was not men's grief, but their joy Christ visited. He worked his first miracle to help men's gladness."

Prayer

Psalm 100

Make a joyful noise to the Lord, all the earth.
Worship the Lord with gladness;
come into his presence with singing.

Know that the Lord is God.
It is he that made us, and we are his;
we are his people, and the sheep of his pasture.

Enter his gates with thanksgiving,
and his courts with praise.
Give thanks to him, bless his name.

For the Lord is good;
his steadfast love endures forever,
and his faithfulness to all generations.

Good Friday began the process
that blasted open the tomb;
Easter Sunday made us "alleluia
people" capable of rejoicing and
singing despite the darkness,
because we're permanently
celebrating such good news.

6

Good Friday Darkness

"For those who believe in Christ, there is no sorrow that is not yet mixed with hope—no despair. There is only a constant being born again, a constant going from darkness to light."
— *Vincent van Gogh*

On the surface this quote from the famous painter, Vincent van Gogh, may seem ironic, since he died at age thirty-seven from a gunshot wound by his own hand. Yet, those who loved him, particularly his brother Theo, saw him as one who deeply cared about others, only to be hurt by them. Ultimately, he was so troubled, so mired in darkness, that he believed he no longer belonged in this world; yet, he was a man who loved others. The evidence of this shines forth in the touching stories of his earlier years, especially when Vincent chose to bring God and humanitarian help to the impoverished workers in the Borinage, a coal-mining region in southwestern Belgium.

Why, then, would van Gogh have killed himself? In his book, *Van Gogh and God,* author Cliff Edwards makes a convincing case that poverty was probably the direct cause of his death. Van Gogh was so poor, such a "financial failure," that Theo, though poor himself and married and with an infant son, supported his older brother. When Theo's baby became ill, van Gogh felt he was a terrible burden, Edwards writes. He wanted to make way "for a child who needed all his parent's resources if he were to survive."

Edwards makes a strong case "that such a man would not have taken his life for any reason but that he felt it was the right thing to do. He believed that he gave his life to save a life—that of his godson—in the spirit of Christ who said, 'Greater love than this no man hath, that he lay down his life for a friend.'" I counter: how much better it might have been if van Gogh had been able to trust that the darkness was *not* his destiny, even as I hope that this man, noted for his compassion, knew that "for those who believe in Christ...there is only a constant being born again, a constant going from darkness to light."

I tell this story because I believe it illustrates so humanly how few people, if any, are spared Good Friday darkness. This is the story of most everyone's life—the Good Fridays where darkness at noon takes over, where all we know is pain and sorrow, falling in and out of despair. I constantly see appearing before me faces of loved ones and friends who were thrown into the darkness, nailed with Christ on that cross, who yet believed they would again see the promised Easter light. There was Jodi, my young sister-in-law, who didn't want fatal breast cancer, but got it; my sister Rosemary, who wished her husband Frank hadn't been the victim of his fatal Parkinson's illness. My co-worker, Virginia, still had plans for her life when lung cancer ended them; my son, Peter, who battled "a missing part" in his brain, as he put it, and lost the fight.

I know so many stories of lives that turned out so differently from the original ideas, hopes, and dreams. These people never chose the Good Friday cross, but they were there all the same, nailed and bleeding in the darkness.

But if we are so trapped in the darkness that we turn away from the rest of the lesson of the cross, then, sadly, the darkness is in danger of becoming permanent. Jesus' suffering and death was about pain, but not despair, because Good Friday, for all its tormenting aura, became the key that opened heaven and left the promise that Light, in the person of Jesus Christ, had conquered darkness.

This is a message and a truth sorely needed to give hope to humankind that suffers so many defeats in this earthly life. If we consider the history of the world to the present, we cannot deny that its overwhelming, apparent story is Good Friday darkness—so much sin, war, brutal evidence of man's inhumanity to man, crimes against and abuse of others. This is the stark evidence of how humanity can lack compassion and love, which are, over and over, the two essential components in Christ's teaching

Jesus said in so many ways that the Creator made us out of love, to *be loving*, which can only be expressed by being compassionate in our relations with others. The message given to us, loud and clear, by the Son was the greatest love story of all time and reached its earthly climax on Good Friday. Yet, at that moment, this became the darkest of days, for no one could have anticipated or understood the rising of the Sun/Son that would promise an end to Good Friday darkness.

None of this can be explained or understood in "worldly" terms. In fact, we are confronting a divine

Lent: An Uncommon Love Story

mystery that is never more paradoxical than during Holy Week. Consider what happens. Jesus is going to be judged guilty and given the death penalty, and his Father isn't going to stop it. In *America* magazine, Jesuit Father Donald Maldari honestly states:

> The role the cross plays in the redemption of the world, though essential, is extremely problematic for us. Traditional explanations of the role of the cross usually include something about a ransom to the Father, a sacrifice and the fulfillment of the Father's will.... But the Father's demand for the Son's gruesome death in order to redeem the world is scandalous. What loving parent, people ask, demands her or his child's death before being willing to fix something that is broken...even if it is the universe.

This priest-professor goes on to underscore that this is a "false image of God" and a "false response" to the radical change in human hearts that was needed to make the world holy again. He emphasizes:

> The only way for Jesus to avoid death would have been to renounce the love that motivated his life and work. Jesus was executed because he refused to stop

loving; he refused to stop challenging the world's status quo. He seems to have known that his mission in life was to love without limits. In his agony in the garden on the night before his execution, he rejected any compromise of that mission. His love conquers evil. Christ's cross redeems the world because it is the love that shines in the darkness, a darkness that cannot overcome it.

Great theologians of the early Church left moving declarations of how God's love shone through the universe precisely because of Good Friday. St. Anselm of Canterbury wrote that "God would not let mankind perish" because of sin and evil. "God's becoming man is the greatest instance of divine mercy." St. Athanasius, the noted third-century bishop, explained:

Man had succumbed, lacking the perseverance to remain in the blissful state the Creator gave.... His creative act was being wasted by man's degeneration. Crucifixion provided the ideal means [to redeem the world] for only by accepting the cross, the form of death prescribed as a curse, could the Word properly bear the curse laid upon man.... The resurrection, by guaranteeing a new beginning to a life now clothed in corruption, gloriously revealed the success of the

Lent: An Uncommon Love Story

How many ways Jesus said it: that
the Creator made us out of love,
to *be loving*, which can only be
expressed by being
compassionate in our relations
with others. The message, given
to us, loud and clear, by the Son,
was the greatest love story of all
time and reached its earthly
climax on Good Friday.

Creator's efforts to free his handiwork from disintegration and to restore it to its pristine condition.

Poets have written of the cataclysmic event: the Good Friday execution overturned by the victory of death, overcome on Easter morning. I have long meditated on these lines by one called only "Anonymous":

And with him hope arose, and life and light.
Men said, "Not Christ, but Death died yesternight."
And joy and truth and all things virtuous
Rose when he rose.

It takes great honesty to look inward to see if we truly love others. Sometimes we need a wake-up call that shines a spotlight on the ways we can delude ourselves in our confidence that we love all as Jesus asks us when we are only giving limited love.

I remember back in the early '70s attending a memorial service for African-American children who had been murdered in Atlanta, Georgia. The speaker told about the sad, personal price paid by people who had lived each day with terror and the threat of ever more terror right in their neighborhoods: "I came home for dinner one day and my wife told me they had found another body in the

Lent: An Uncommon Love Story

river. 'Is that so?' I commented, and I went right on eating." "This is the new tragedy," he continued, his voice rising. "We have no more tears!"

He said it had become normal in those days of the Civil Rights turmoil to see hearses go by, to hear mothers crying. But when something happens so often, over a long period of time, people lose their sensitivity. His voice grew even louder, and, sounding like a preacher, he declared, "I want to share my new prayer with you today. If the Lord can't deliver us from the horror and the pain, I ask that he at least send us more tears, because if we can't cry, then we have stopped feeling!"

I was affected by this man's words because I recognized myself in them. I had read about the murdered children, said "how terrible," and prayed for their families. But I had not cried for them. Much later, after so much of my own pain, especially from the deaths of loved ones, I had cried more tears than could ever be counted. That's when I really understood that tears are about love—that love for everyone who has ever been given life, the love that was bursting from Christ on the cross on that Good Friday, no conditions, no restrictions. When we join our tears with his, we are on our way out of the Good Friday darkness, ready to follow Christ to the new light where we now understand that life is eternal because it originates in God's love.

It was certainly not accidental, but by divine plan, that Jesus spoke so strongly to his disciples about love in those last hours before he sweat blood in the Garden of Olives, seeking his Father's help and strength before surrendering to the Roman executioners. He had told them all along to love God above all and "your neighbor as yourself." And, hard to believe, he had insisted that they love their enemies. Then when his hour had come, he told those he had chosen to carry on his work to "love one another as I have loved you."

Jesus told them, firmly, that he gave them unconditional love so that they would learn, in turn, to give unconditional love to others. Yet neither the disciples then nor we now would ever have learned to give unconditional love to others without Christ. To do this, he had to die and rise from the dead—so that he could resurrect within each one of us. That's why his Father didn't stay the execution. Jesus, his Son, was the Father's gift.

The Father gave us an extraordinary gift when he sent his Son into our world. It was the gift of letting us know that we are never alone, for we are all related to each other in him and in his Son. We know this truth as the "Communion of Saints," a wonderful doctrine all too often glossed over or ignored. I began thinking more deeply about this truth when I happened to come across an old book, one that I wished I had read when I was a science major in college and began hearing claims that the great advances of science would soon make religion irrelevant. In this book, *Love and the Law,* author Fenwicke L. Holmes countered a growing assertion that "The old faith and the new science cannot dwell together in unity." He asked, "Can we show that the *ultimate* of science is but the introduction to God? I feel we can."

Fenwicke found the answer in Jesus' personal magnetism and enthusiasm. He wrote that "The virile energy of the fingers of science feeling out the wonders of God's nature is charged with the dynamics of Jesus' enthusiasm...the outpouring of the boundless life of God." He further predicted that science itself would one day help us "know the divinity within us."

I felt a strange connection to this author when I checked the date of publication. Fenwicke wrote his book in 1928, when I was two weeks old. Could he ever have imagined that a baby born as his book went to print would, some seventy years later, find inspiration in it and be grateful to him, who so long ago affirmed that God was and ever would be the author of all science? Truly, this is the way the Communion of Saints works in God's plan. We find solace, learning, help, and so much more because we are all connected to one another, always sharing the life of our heavenly Creator.

After my sons Peter and John died, I came to understand the true wonder and joy of this spiritual "bonding." So many people called and wrote, expressing their sadness—and their tears—for me. Our "communion" existed because it came directly from the cross, and I saw as I never had before that the life, death, and resurrection of our Lord Jesus had insured us that never again would we be alone in our sufferings.

Those letters and calls gave me a strengthened understanding of what it means to be part of the Church community. No matter how many losses we suffer, no matter the degree of pain we must endure, we are not alone—we never have been, because of baptism, which St. Paul tells us makes us part of one body: Christ's.

One night, when I was in such agony over the deaths of my sons, I was praying for some solace. I suddenly received an image of the head of Christ on the cross, as he may have looked at 3 P.M. on Good Friday. Then the image changed, and instead of the crown of thorns, I saw our Lord wearing a gold, shining crown. I believe the Lord was giving me the solace of "seeing" that Good Friday had the happiest ending imaginable. I then understood in a more intense way than ever before what Jesus meant when he spoke of his *joy*. It was that of a darkness transformed into light.

Since then I have often turned to Psalm 61, which gives us assurance of God's protection. How could I doubt it again?

Prayer

Psalm 61

Hear my cry, O God;
>> listen to my prayer.
From the end of the earth I call to you,
>> when my heart is faint.

Lead me to the rock
>> that is higher than I;
for you are my refuge,
>> a strong tower against the enemy.

Let me abide in your tent forever,
     find refuge under the shelter of your wings.
For you, O God, have heard my vows;
     you have given me the heritage of those who fear
          your name.

Prolong the life of the king;
     may his years endure to all generations!
May he be enthroned forever before God;
     appoint steadfast love and faithfulness to watch
          over him!

So I will always sing praises to your name,
     as I pay my vows day after day.

Jesus' suffering and death was
about pain, but not despair,
because Good Friday, for all its
tormenting aura, became the key
that opened heaven and left the
promise that Light, in the person
of Jesus Christ, had conquered
darkness.

The Power Flowing from Easter

"If Christ be not risen, then is our preaching vain, and your faith is also vain."
— *St. Paul*

For over 2,000 years the story of Jesus' rising from the tomb has remained a subject running the gamut of speculation and debate among non-believers of the Christian faith. Yet, for believers, this was the Easter morning miracle that became "the turning point of history...a new creation bursting in on the old," as expressed by N. T. Wright. On Friday, Jesus had died, for all people knew at that moment, this man, the hoped-for Messiah, was simply a failure, or worse, a fraud. Yet, in the days and years to come, "why did people go on talking about Jesus of Nazareth, except as a remarkable but tragic memory?" Wright immediately answers, because "Jesus was raised from the dead.... The resurrection...was the only reason why his life and words possessed any relevance two weeks, let alone two millennia, after his death."

Nearly a hundred years ago the study of Jesus captivated another researcher, Cambridge scholar, T. R. Glover, whose book, *Jesus of History,* offered this conclusion:

Take away the resurrection, however it happened, whatever it was, and the history of the Church is unintelligible. We live in a rational world—a world where, however much remains as yet unexplained, everything has a promise of being lucid.... Great results have great causes. We have to find, somewhere or other, between crucifixion and the first preaching of the disciples in Jerusalem, something that entirely changed the character of that group of men.

He went on:

Something happened, so tremendous and so vital, that it changed not only the character of the movement and the men—but with them, the whole history of the world.... When it came to the cross, his cross, they ran away. A few weeks later we find them rejoicing to be beaten, imprisoned, and put to death. What had happened? What we have to explain is a new

Lent: An Uncommon Love Story

life—a new life of prayer and joy and *power*...in a new relation to God.

The events of that weekend from Friday to Sunday 2,000 years ago were beyond incredible. People who knew Jesus saw him hanging on the cross, exposed and exhausted, with his life's blood slowly draining away from the beatings, the nails, and the gash in his side. If "seeing is believing," there could be no doubt: he was dead. And with their spirits matching his lifelessness, the followers of Jesus—betrayed, disillusioned, abandoned, and hopeless—buried him.

Yet, not too many hours later, he was gone from his tomb. It could have been a trick, a bad joke, or the best magic show in town.

It was none of these. It was for real.

At first his followers didn't know the elation that all "winners" feel. With his death, they had thought all was lost. They didn't know they would soon be energized by a power as yet unknown to the world. This power would be given to them by their leader, who had demonstrated that he was the greatest friend, prophet, link to God they could have imagined—first by his life, then by his death overcome, and then as he returned to them. True, there were Caesars, there would be kings and Napoleons who would one day rule by might and force and be called powerful. But in every case, their power would end. Their power was fleeting, transitory, and, finally, empty, because, without exception, when each died their power also died.

Jesus, like no one before, proved he had the ultimate power, the control over his death. He could rule forever because no earthly force could make his death permanent. The conquering of death was indeed his Easter message. He came back, proving the truth of his promise: "I am with you always." He kept his promise to his followers that he would be with them "to the end of time."

What had been hard for Jesus' followers to understand was his refusal to exercise the kind of earthly power that men and women have always understood—the power that makes people cringe and obey, that puts some humans in control of others, that programs the structures within which we live, work, and die.

During his life and ministry, Jesus' criteria for power was decidedly unusual. Power was not to be lumped together with controlling others by force or might. Jesus brought power back to basics. Power originated with life and had to do with how people controlled their own lives—from within. It therefore had to be as universal as life itself. Power belonged to everyone. So, what kind of power did Jesus initiate on Easter?

It was a power as fundamental as the force which had produced life along with every support that life needs to exist and renew itself. Jesus stated it time and again: Love is the real power. Love is the only thing we can take with us not just to death but beyond.

Love adds the essential quality to life that can put a person beyond the limited everyday conditions of existence. Even when despots ruled, or illness struck, or there were no jobs, love would be the way in which people could control their lives from the inside. Love takes life out of the realm of endless individual cycles and makes it intermingled, connected, and continuous, joining all people as relatives, not opponents or adversaries. It has the power to give people happiness and purpose, to make them special—whether they be slaves or kings.

That message was hard to understand when Christ first spoke it, and still is, unless we think of it in terms of its opposite—the absence of love, which is a sterile, cold, frightening place where individual value simply doesn't exist. Jesus couldn't promise spectacular results from this strange brand of power because it was being injected into a world that wants an instant, see-it-now payoff, a me-centered and violence-prone world. But he came to earth to bring his Father's message about true power: people have no power when they latch on to things that are destined to end. Jesus had come to show us his Father's plan for us, demonstrating the powerful pay-off for those who follow him—life forever.

So many people have discovered this power in the past 2,000 years. Some have started at a zero point, like Greta Palmer, an atheist who worked as a journalist and war correspondent during World War II. She had to report on the violence that still shatters nations and people to the death in war. Yet, time and time again, she was humbled and astounded at finding incredible nobility and unselfishness in the exhausted soldiers who shared what little they had with poor, bewildered civilians.

Palmer kept asking herself, "Where does it come from, this light in the eyes of combat soldiers?" She saw this light as a power that had come from somewhere, and she wanted to be connected to this power. Her yearning drew her to Jesus and the Catholic Church after she read the

During his life and ministry, Jesus' criteria for power was decidedly unusual. Power was not to be lumped together with controlling others, by force or might. Jesus brought power back to basics...as fundamental as the force which had produced life along with every support that life needs to exist and renew itself. Jesus stated it time and again: Love.

words of the British author, G. K. Chesterton, a Catholic convert: "The Church is not a movement, but a meeting place, the trysting place of all the truths in the world." The basic truth for Chesterton was that God sent us his Son "to show us how to make the world right."

As Greta Palmer searched to discover these truths for herself, she found the answer to her question about the soldiers. The "light" in their eyes had come from God. She sought that light, yearning to make it her own light, and found it in Jesus Christ, who revealed his Father to her and led her to the Catholic Church. No wonder she could affirm, "The Catholic God is not 2,000 years away. He is as close as this second."

For some twenty centuries now, people have been discovering this same truth, giving evidence of the power that will always flow from the Easter Sunday miracle.

The followers of Christ had a lot to learn after that first Sunday. Being human and knowing only their limited world, the disciples had at times looked for a "get-even" power while they were moved to follow Jesus. As Luke reports in his Gospel, when a Samaritan village refused to receive Jesus, his disciples, James and John, asked, "Lord, do you want us to command fire to come down from heaven and consume them?" (Lk 9:54).... Jesus rebuked them. Jesus had no intention of taking over the world in the usual fashion of physical might and worldly power. Because his kingdom was not of this world, not experienced through the eyes but through the spirit, he chose to exercise a power that was also not of this world. His power could only be experienced through the spirit, not the eyes and the sword.

Because of this, love, a power springing from God, the Source of life, can never be ended by men and women. It can never self-destruct. Love will remain always the lasting power, magnificently "on call" to give nobility to every person who sees the power-message of Easter, hears its invitation, and says, "Yes!"

Years ago I found a long sentence that I copied on a piece of paper and stuck in a file I call "Inspiration." It said: "Pentecost means power—power to forgive injuries, to keep an un-soured spirit amid the deepest injustices, to overcome evil with good, hate by love, and the world by a cross."

That was the first time I had ever associated Pentecost—Easter's powerful sequel—with power. I held long-lasting suspicions about that word power. I had seen too many negative fallouts, which I perceived as resulting from power, from how decisions are made by people in control—decisions that bring on wars, break up families, ignore the poor, harm the environment....

It was a new inspiration to consider that it takes power to forgive injuries and overcome evil, as that long-cherished quote affirmed. Not that I hadn't often considered power's meaning. I remember being asked to give a talk on power to a women's group back in the '70s. I made many notes for myself, beginning with "how we define power is crucial...underscore that power is a complex issue because it permeates all aspects of our life...go back to its root meaning—that power is not force, might, or clout. It means 'to be able,' has to do with potential." My words were upbeat, even when I had to acknowledge how careful we must be to recognize when others are using their power to pull us down.

Reviewing these notes, I found a quote about power from well-known psychologist, Rollo May:

> Power is the birthright of every human being. It is the source of his self-esteem and the root of his conviction that he is interpersonally significant. Whether a

Lent: An Uncommon Love Story

person is black or a woman or a convict or a patient in a mental hospital...the problem (of power) is roughly the same—to enable the individual to feel he will be counted, that "attention will be paid."

Reading his words again thirty years later I find I relate differently to them. For I have learned that the deep tragedies I have undergone were bearable only because they weren't the whole picture. I have been blessed with great joys, too, and love has given me the power to survive. Dr. May's words about power struck me with a new force. For I have come to believe, with certainty, that the individual has, indeed, been counted, and yes, attention has been paid. The price was steep—high as a cross on a Friday—yet freely given to us in love on a Sunday. So why have we not understood this power, the legacy of love given to everyone at Easter?

Sadly, because power has so often been misused by the inhabitants of this world. Evil has seduced so many with the grand lie that it is better to aim for earthly power, because that kind of power can control others. Jesus, instead, offered us the truth that all power comes from his Father, meaning that the only true power is to be "one" with him and his Father. When we choose—because of our God-given free will—to relate to others, not with anger, meanness, or demeaning criticism, but with compassion, forgiveness, and love, as the Father would, *then* we have the power that matters, the spiritual power of the Risen Lord in us.

In the Gospel of John, Pilate confronts Jesus, who will not answer his questions. He asks him, "Do you refuse to speak to me? Do you not know that I have power to release you, and power to crucify you?" And Jesus responds, "You would have no power over me unless it had been given you from above" (Jn 19:10–11).

What followed was the death penalty for Jesus, who was then hammered to a cross and held there, not by Roman nails, but by love, to his last breath.

Jesus didn't have to die in agony, an apparently powerless man. He could have preached eloquently on evil, pain, and hardships, telling us that, in the end, all will be okay because our Father in heaven loves us. But people, themselves suffering and in pain, would have said, "Prove it!" and then walked away. Jesus could have left us a great teaching about how we don't really die, that after earthly death we are resurrected to new life because our Father in heaven loves us. But no one would have believed him.

Lent: An Uncommon Love Story

Jesus couldn't just proclaim these truths. He had to prove to us that he was telling the truth. He loved us enough to do this by enduring human torture, human death, and then taking the final step—leaving the tomb, proving his power to conquer evil, pain, and death. We are the inheritors of this power that shook the world on Easter. We received our inheritance on Pentecost, fifty days later.

While I was doing extensive research for a book I was writing on World War II, I found an unexpected confirmation of all I had ever come to understand about why Jesus had to die for us. It was a poem by an unknown soldier who had been killed—a poem which he entitled "Resurrection." Its last verse explains so very well the power of Easter:

> If death ends all, then evil must be good,
> Wrong must be right, and beauty ugliness.
> God is a Judas who betrays his Son
> And, with a kiss damns all the world to hell—
> If Christ rose not again.

The joyful song of Psalm 98 is so fitting in remembering the great power of the Lord given to all of us forever on Easter morning:

The Lord has made known his victory;
   he has revealed his vindication in the sight of
      the nations.
He has remembered his steadfast love and
      faithfulness
   to the house of Israel.
All the ends of the earth have seen
   the victory of our God.

Let the floods clap their hands;
   let the hills sing together for joy
at the presence of the Lord...(vv. 2–3, 8–9).

Prayer

Psalm 98

O sing to the LORD a new song,
   for he has done marvelous things.
His right hand and his holy arm
   have gotten him victory.
The LORD has made known his victory;
      he has revealed his vindication in the sight of the
         nations.

He has remembered his steadfast love and faithfulness
    to the house of Israel.
All the ends of the earth have seen
    the victory of our God.

Make a joyful noise to the LORD, all the earth;
    break forth into joyous song and sing praises.
Sing praises to the LORD with the lyre,
    with the lyre and the sound of melody.
With trumpets and the sound of the horn
    make a joyful noise before the King, the LORD.

Let the sea roar, and all that fills it;
    the world and those who live in it.
Let the floods clap their hands;
    let the hills sing together for joy
at the presence of the LORD, for he is coming
    to judge the earth.
He will judge the world with righteousness,
    and the peoples with equity.

Conclusion

I have spent more hours than I could count thinking of what Lent has meant to me in the years of my life, and I find myself incredibly grateful to Sr. Madonna, an editor I highly respect, who offered me the opportunity to share what I have studied and learned personally about this time in our Church year. Now I offer a few closing thoughts.

I honestly acknowledge that when I was much younger, I was somewhat critical of the idea of Ash Wednesday because I thought it had a dreariness about it. The idea of "dust we are and to dust we shall return" almost seemed to defy the truth of resurrection and eternal life. That sentence didn't seem very hopeful or life affirming.

But as the years went on, I came to see there is a good reason behind this idea of ashes. It tells us that we must face our earthly mortality, our vulnerability to weakness, our moral failures. That's our human condition. That's reality. And so we need to "repent" and "heal" so we can get up and seek with vigor what is ultimately important.

If we open our hearts, we learn how Lent—that dry time in the desert for forty days—has a happy ending. Lent invites us to meet again the Person who knows us, loves us, and can give us enduring life. The climax of the Lenten story is Easter, when Jesus Christ brings us out of Lent and to eternal life because he is eternal love itself. This is the most astounding love story ever lived.

Before we get to this understanding, however, we may question why there has to be the Ash Wednesday emphasis on dust and ashes—especially when we have to explain this to our children and grandchildren! Well, it comes from the Bible, from Genesis. "Then the Lord formed man from the dust of the ground, and breathed into his nostrils the breath of life and the man became a living being."

I wonder if we ever think about that line, really. God could have made us from starlight or sun rays, from clouds or wind. But he made humans from dust. I think God made us from the earth so we'd always know we are one with all creation. He insured that we'd get that message in a very plain and striking way—by making us out of earth.

Over the years, I studied a lot of science and learned that nothing in nature dies "completely." Everything lives again in one form or another. We breathe because God put his breath in us, as he put breath in all of nature. Because we're made from earth, we should be able to identify with how nature hangs on to life, and so be able to believe that this is our destiny, too—to be reborn after dying, to live again.

Resurrection is the great theme of nature. How great a God it is who made all his creation for eternal life!

Yet, enter sin, and with its emphasis on darkness and mortality and ashes. And so we need Ash Wednesday and Lent to jolt us to "repent" and focus again on our great origins and our destiny of eternal life, designed by the Father, guaranteed by the life and death of the Son, and continually energized by the Holy Spirit.

Lent is only the prelude; God made us for the prize— Easter.

BOOKS & MEDIA

The Daughters of St. Paul operate book and media centers at the following addresses. Visit, call or write the one nearest you today, or find us on the World Wide Web, www.pauline.org

CALIFORNIA

3908 Sepulveda Blvd, Culver City, CA 90230	310-397-8676
5945 Balboa Avenue, San Diego, CA 92111	858-565-9181
46 Geary Street, San Francisco, CA 94108	415-781-5180

FLORIDA

145 S.W. 107th Avenue, Miami, FL 33174	305-559-6715

HAWAII

1143 Bishop Street, Honolulu, HI 96813	808-521-2731
Neighbor Islands call:	800-259-8463

ILLINOIS

172 North Michigan Avenue, Chicago, IL 60601	312-346-4228

LOUISIANA

4403 Veterans Memorial Blvd, Metairie, LA 70006	504-887-7631

MASSACHUSETTS

885 Providence Hwy, Dedham, MA 02026	781-326-5385

MISSOURI

9804 Watson Road, St. Louis, MO 63126	314-965-3512

NEW JERSEY

561 U.S. Route 1, Wick Plaza, Edison, NJ 08817	732-572-1200

NEW YORK

150 East 52nd Street, New York, NY 10022	212-754-1110
78 Fort Place, Staten Island, NY 10301	718-447-5071

PENNSYLVANIA

9171-A Roosevelt Blvd, Philadelphia, PA 19114	215-676-9494

SOUTH CAROLINA

243 King Street, Charleston, SC 29401	843-577-0175

TENNESSEE

4811 Poplar Avenue, Memphis, TN 38117	901-761-2987

TEXAS

114 Main Plaza, San Antonio, TX 78205	210-224-8101

VIRGINIA

1025 King Street, Alexandria, VA 22314	703-549-3806

CANADA

3022 Dufferin Street, Toronto, ON M6B 3T5	416-781-9131

¡También somos su fuente para libros, videos y música en español!